LinkedIn
FOR THE
SAVVY
EXECUTIVE

PROMOTE
YOUR BRAND
WITH
AUTHENTICITY,
TACT AND
POWER

Carol J. Kaemmerer

ARTISAN
DIGITAL

www.ArtisanDigitalAgency.com
(651) 600-0178

PRAISE FOR
LINKEDIN FOR THE
SAVVY EXECUTIVE

"So many executives I meet today are having a hard time finding the time to capitalize on all the great features of LinkedIn. Carol Kaemmerer has done a great job in narrowing down "all the things" to "the most important things" you should be doing on LinkedIn to get real results. She shares those features and techniques in her easy to read, very actionable book, *LinkedIn for the Savvy Executive.*"

Wayne Breitbarth
Professional Speaker, Trainer, Consultant and Author of
*The Power Formula for LinkedIn Success: Kick-Start Your
Business, Brand and Job Search*

"I am the most fervent believer that LinkedIn is a game-changer in the world of personal branding and a must-have for every career-minded executive. *LinkedIn for the Savvy Executive* is an outstanding resource for professionals who want to use LinkedIn to expand their brand visibility, stand out from the competition and attract the attention of decision-makers and influencers."

William Arruda
Bestselling author of the definitive books on personal branding: *Career Distinction* and *Ditch. Dare. Do!*

"As a business executive, key executive advisor, consultant and mentor, Carol Kaemmerer's expertise is fully reflected in her book. She provides critical rationale as to why it is imperative for today's executive to showcase their skills and talents so that the right people and opportunities find them. *LinkedIn for the Savvy Executive* is a wonderful blend of strategy, practical use of LinkedIn features, and solid branding advice to help you reflect who you are and what differentiates you from others. This is a must read for all… especially, those in transition or contemplating a move!"

John F. Ruppel
Vice President, Lee Hecht Harrison & Principal of J.F. Ruppel & Associates (Sr. Executive Coaching Firm)

"Carol cuts through all the hoopla over why LinkedIn is so great to the practical know-how of what your profile should look like to open new doors and solidify current contacts. If you want to boost your business savvy, give yourself the gift of Carol in a book."

Roshini Rajkumar
Presence Engineer, Speaker and Author of *Communicate That!*

"I believe that words can create reality. Through her active listening and powerful positioning words, Carol helped me enhance my personal brand as a family business advisor, providing momentum to my practice. This book cannot channel all of the benefits of Carol's executive coaching and profile development, but her emphasis on strategy for executives and her clear, accessible writing style make this a must-read for executives who take responsibility for their career direction."

Eric Gustafson
Managing Partner and
Family Business Advisor, Gustafson Group

"*LinkedIn for the Savvy Executive* is accessible and actionable for the busy executive. While LinkedIn books generally focus on mechanics, Carol Kaemmerer focuses instead on strategies, helping the executive reader understand how to use LinkedIn in ways that are consistent with their personal brand. I've made changes to my profile already and have a list of things still to address. Executives, this is a great read."

Lori Syverson
President, Edina Chamber of Commerce

"Carol Kaemmerer has created a wonderful resource for executives looking to ramp up their presence on LinkedIn. I especially appreciated the chapter on profile pictures, which is spot on. Great work!"

Jennifer Kelly
Photographer and Owner, KeliComm Headshots

"*LinkedIn for the Savvy Executive* is the best kind of how-to – it is also **why-to**. My favorite part of the book addresses why executives need LinkedIn. The data on executive mobility should move any executive away from the "I don't have time for LinkedIn" stance to active engagement with this now-essential social medium. This book is well worth the investment of time."

Sally Stockbridge, SPHR, SHRM-SCP
Human Resources Leader and Consultant

"When you read this book, it's like Carol Kaemmerer is sitting there discussing strategy with you and explaining why it works. Carol was my LinkedIn coach and it seems to me that she's actually giving away her seed corn here in this book. It's your gain. Read it and reap."

Kurt Grotenhuis, CPA
Managing Partner and Principal Consultant,
KURT Konsulting

"In her book *LinkedIn for the Savvy Executive*, Carol Kaemmerer has addressed many of the questions we hear from the executives we coach at Navigate Forward. Her tone, style and information are spot on for the executive audience. I enjoyed the read and learned a few things myself."

Mary Kloehn
COO and President, Navigate Forward

"'Do I need to be on Linkedin at my level? In my industry? With my tenure?' If you're an executive in today's employment market, chances are good the answer to these questions is a resounding 'Yes!' *LinkedIn for the Savvy Executive* will put you on the path to a highly successful profile and presence on today's most important online professional network."

Sue Plaster, M.Ed.
Diversity, Leadership, Succession Planning and
Individual Job Search Consultant, Sue Plaster Consulting

"Carol Kaemmerer is a ***master*** at LinkedIn coaching for executives, and at writing about LinkedIn strategy in a way we can all understand. She's just published your next reading assignment – *LinkedIn for the Savvy Executive*. This is your chance to have an expert perched on your shoulder as you establish and enhance your own LinkedIn profile and presence!"

Richard Dodson
Creative Career Catalyst, Speaker and Author of
Power Your Career: The Art of Tactful Self-Promotion at Work

"Carol has provided me a wealth of insight regarding my LinkedIn profile and how to message my experiences and accomplishments. When I get asked about how my messaging is so impactful I immediately recognize Carol for her efforts and connect that person with her. I have had a number of people that I've sent her way come back to me with tremendous gratitude for helping them."

Tony Fisher
Retail Executive and Entrepreneur

"I've worked with Carol over many years because she is masterful at communicating difficult-to-understand material in a manner that is accessible to a wide variety of audiences. So it comes as no surprise to me that her book on LinkedIn is well researched, well argued, well written – and well worth the read. I highly recommend it."

Bob Thompson, MPA, MS
President, Comprehensive Reimbursement Solutions

"If you want to be seen as a thought leader in your industry or profession – and what executive doesn't? – you need to be social media savvy. Carol does a superb job of making the case for using LinkedIn well, not just for executives, but for any career-minded person. Every executive reader will take away something valuable from this book."

Nancy Burke
Principal, Burke & Penn, and Author of
Power Your Career: The Art of Tactful Self-Promotion at Work

FOREWORD

THERE ARE MANY how-to books about LinkedIn. This is not one of them. I don't want you to get lost in the mechanics of the platform, which change frequently and without warning.

Rather, this book will provide strategies for executives to use LinkedIn with authenticity, tact and power. I want you to understand the importance of this essential social media platform for your career, both now and in the future. I'd like to help you control the way you present yourself on LinkedIn through your profile and online interactions.

> This book will provide strategies for executives to use LinkedIn with authenticity, tact and power.

When your LinkedIn profile highlights your business story with passion and authenticity, you attract your ideal customers, clients, employers and employees – those who resonate with your message.

Beyond just housing your profile, LinkedIn is a relationship-building tool – an efficient way to engage with those you care about in your business. LinkedIn is also a vehicle for expressing your thought leadership, building your own brand as a leader and contributing to your company's brand equity.

This book will guide you, the savvy executive, to use LinkedIn in a way that powers your career.

AUTHOR'S NOTE

I WROTE THIS BOOK with the intention that you would read it from cover to cover. The key concepts are best understood when read from start to finish.

But if you are a person who wishes to read selectively, both the Table of Contents and the final assessment (*in Chapter 11: Bringing It All Together*) may help you choose areas you'd like to read first.

A caveat: **Do not make changes to your LinkedIn profile until you have read Chapter Four**, because some of LinkedIn's default settings can make you appear very un-savvy indeed.

The language I use to describe LinkedIn's settings and functions is the current terminology as it appears on the computer. LinkedIn apps available for phone and tablets may use different terminology and offer limited functionality, so I suggest you change your settings from your computer.

CONTENTS

CHAPTER 1

WHY DO EXECUTIVES NEED LINKEDIN?

> **If I google you and find nothing, then at best you are a very unremarkable person.**
>
> DAVE PARNELL

BASED ON MY EXPERIENCE as an Executive Branding Coach, most executives have very poor LinkedIn profiles. They often have a good photo (thanks to their corporate communications department), 500+ connections (because everyone wants to connect with them) and a default headline (that LinkedIn provides based on their current title and company). Also, they've listed their current position and where they went to school. Beyond that, their profiles tend to be incomplete and lacking customization. Why is that? And more importantly, why does it matter?

Here are the reasons I hear most frequently from executives about why their profiles are so bare:

- "I thought that LinkedIn was just for job seekers."
- "I wasn't aware that a great profile could attract one's ideal customers, partners and potential employees."
- "I don't actually know how LinkedIn works and I don't want to look foolish by using the medium poorly."

While deciding not to use LinkedIn might have been an option a few years ago, it simply will not work going forward. People check you out on LinkedIn before they meet you – people including potential business partners, customers and the talent your company hopes to attract. Today's executive will not look current without a stellar LinkedIn presence. While some view LinkedIn as an online résumé, the platform is so much more. It is an awesome database that can be mined effectively for business purposes. It is a tool for brand building and online interaction. And it is a vehicle that can help you be found – for partnering with others, for board nominations, for internal task forces, for succession planning and for exciting new opportunities beyond your current company.

> Today's executive will not look current without a stellar LinkedIn presence.

Executives who have a stellar LinkedIn presence find that it helps them to:

- leverage corporate or product brand and improve brand visibility
- establish thought leadership
- build quality relationships, both online and face-to-face
- prepare for meetings by researching the background of attendees
- search for top talent, leads, potential collaborators/partners, etc.
- attract and retain top talent
- demonstrate leadership and track record
- attract those who might buy from or partner with your company
- nurture relationships with investors, shareholders, employees and other stakeholders

It also helps executives with their own career mobility. Regardless of how secure your tenure may seem, nothing lasts forever. The Executive Mobility Report, 2013, conducted by Blue Steps found:

- 44% of senior level executives are with the same company for only two to five years
- 55% of senior level executives have worked for two to three organizations at the senior level
- 76% of senior level executives are willing to make a career transition immediately for the right opportunity

Executives with an up-to-date LinkedIn profile can be found – both internally (for task force appointments, succession planning, etc.) and externally (for not-for-profit and paid board positions, and corporate executive opportunities).

> Every savvy executive needs a dynamite LinkedIn presence.

Resources

Blue Steps, *Executive Mobility Report, 2013.* "How Long Is Executive Tenure?"

Rich Smith, "The LinkedIn Effect: Why Social Media Is Now Mandatory for Success." *Forbes,* October 14, 2014.

CHAPTER 2

WHAT'S **EXECUTIVE** GOT TO DO WITH IT?

> "Everything you do affects your brand. It's up to you to determine whether your brand is affected positively or negatively."
>
> PETER SHANKMAN

ALTHOUGH THE IDEA of "executive presence" is elusive, it is a palpable phenomenon embodying poise, confidence and professionalism – blended with charisma or a "wow" factor. As an expert at the top of your field, you want to put forth a solid executive presence, not only in person, but also online.

Behaviors that indicate executive presence include:

- using clear language
- speaking with passion and energy
- displaying positive body language (standing straight, making eye contact, offering a firm handshake)
- using an authoritative tone of voice
- being able to command a room – when you speak, others listen

There are perhaps as many ways to express one's executive presence as there are executives. Here are a few. I'm sure you can think of others, based on your own and others' style.

EMOTIONAL CONNECTION

Executives who are emotionally available relate extremely well to their employees. They may make it a point to know and use employees' names. Recall the photo of President Obama greeting a janitor at the White House with a fist bump and smile. One executive I know sends handwritten notes on distinctive stationery to recognize employee accomplishments. Another is fully present in the moment, giving total attention to whomever he's with.

PHYSICAL PRESENCE

Some executives are physically commanding. Think of erect posture and a natural grace; or an unerring sense of style, impeccable grooming and a dazzling smile. These are people who everyone spots instantly when they enter a room. Think of former Secretaries of State General Colin Powell or Madeleine Albright.

INTELLECTUAL PROWESS

Those who express their executive presence with strong intellect are widely recognized for their knowledge and expertise. Picture theoretical physicist and cosmologist Stephen Hawking or Secretary of State Henry Kissinger.

VISIONARY POWER

Executives who present as visionaries enlist others to their overarching worldview. They slice through complex ideas with a single, clear message. Call to mind Steve Jobs and his "think different" mantra.

However it is defined and expressed, executive presence is something that companies are looking for in their executives. In a recent study from the research organization, Center for Talent Innovation, the senior executives surveyed indicated that "being *perceived* as leadership material" was essential to being promoted into a leadership position and accounted for 26% of what it takes to be promoted.

According to the Center for Talent Innovation study, things that detract from executive presence include mistakes such as an unkempt appearance or ill-fitting cloth-ing (cited by 75% of the senior executives surveyed) and sounding uneducated (cited by 60%).

How does all this tie to LinkedIn?

We typically think of executive presence as something that is observable when the executive is in the room. But your executive presence, that blend of charisma and polish, can also shine through your LinkedIn presence. Likewise, mistakes in your profile and the way you use the platform can diminish your personal brand.

> But your executive presence, that blend of charisma and polish, can also shine through your LinkedIn presence. Likewise, mistakes in your profile and the way you use the platform can diminish your personal brand.

Everything in your executive LinkedIn profile reflects on you, your personal brand – and if you are currently employed, on your company's brand as well. So your profile must be complete and free of misspellings and grammatical errors. It must also communicate with power, clarity and authenticity to create an emotional connection between the reader and you, the executive. There is power in being real – in sharing who you truly are.

Your trademark attributes can also shine through (or be tarnished by) how you use the platform. For example, if you are an executive who makes it a point to know employees by name, you would be expected to respond positively to a connection request from any employee in your company.

While it is true that the format for an executive LinkedIn profile is no different from the format for others, the standard by which an executive profile is judged is much higher. Likewise, the way an executive uses LinkedIn to add value to others, cultivate relationships and establish thought leadership should be an extension of the way they conduct themselves in person. (*We will explore how to do that in Chapter Five.*)

> Think about the way in which you demonstrate your executive presence. How will you reflect that in…
>
> - your LinkedIn profile?
> - the way you connect and interact with others online?
> - the way you cultivate your thought leadership online?

Resources

Jenna Goudreu, "Do You Have 'Executive Presence?'" *Forbes*, October 29, 2012.

Sylvia Ann Hewlett, *Executive Presence: The Missing Link Between Merit and Success.* New York: HarperCollins Books, 2014.

Sylvia Ann Hewlett, Lauren Leader-Chivée, Laura Sherbin, Joanne Gordon & Fabiola Dieudonné, "Executive Presence: Key Findings," *Center for Talent Innovation*, November 2012.

Cindy Wahler, "Six Behavioral Traits That Define Executive Presence," *Forbes*, July 2, 2015.

CHAPTER 3

YOUR EXECUTIVE-BRANDED LINKEDIN PORTRAIT

How you look

How you speak

+ How you act

─────────────

Your personal brand

WHEN SOMEONE LOOKS at your LinkedIn profile, your portrait is what initially captures their eye. It's as though they are meeting you for the first time. Appearance counts. While an average photo is sufficient for most people, as a savvy executive, your photo should visually convey your personal brand. In your photo you need to appear to make eye contact with the viewer and project a polished and approachable image.

Don't even consider not using a photo on LinkedIn. Although your photo doesn't influence your ranking on a LinkedIn keyword search, it has everything to do with whether your profile is opened. LinkedIn research tells us that people who have portraits are 21 times more likely to have their profiles opened than people who do not.

Don't even consider not using a photo on LinkedIn.

In your photo, you should be smiling, or at least looking approachable. As the best-selling author and motivational speaker Denis Waitley has said, "A smile is the light in your window that tells others that there is a caring, sharing person inside."

People size you up in seconds. Amy Cuddy, a Harvard Business School professor who has spent years studying first impressions, says that on a first encounter people quickly answer two questions:

- Can I trust this person?
- Can I respect this person?

In particular, people evaluate you on the dimensions of *warmth* and *competence*. Cuddy notes that even in a professional context people's first evaluation is on your warmth or trustworthiness; competence is evaluated only after trust is established.

Knowing the importance of your portrait in conveying your personal brand, take a look at your currently posted photo and determine whether it is serving you well. Here are some prompts to help you decide whether you need a new photo. Even one positive response means it's time for an update:

- ☐ Someone other than a professional photographer took your picture.
- ☐ Your spouse (or significant other or trusted colleague) says something like "it's so-so" or "well, it does *look* like you…"
- ☐ Your face is not in sharp focus.
- ☐ It is obvious that someone was cropped out of your photo.
- ☐ Your photo does not fill the full, square LinkedIn frame or has insufficient resolution (perhaps because you are trying to make a headshot from a full-body shot).
- ☐ Your current photo is a full-body shot.
- ☐ Something else in the photo is more captivating than you are.
- ☐ Your five o'clock shadow is showing or your face has an unflattering sheen.
- ☐ A glare on your glasses obscures your eyes or you are wearing sunglasses.

☐ You are not making eye contact with the camera.

☐ You are not smiling or you do not look approachable.

☐ You are wearing clothes that you wouldn't wear to a board presentation.

☐ The color or fit of your clothes does not flatter you.

☐ The background is not complimentary or looks cheap.

☐ Your expression is grim or stern; you are squinting or frowning; you look unhappy or in pain.

☐ The lighting is not flattering.

☐ You have a halo of light surrounding your head.

☐ The photo is not in color (B&W and sepia-toned photos do not hold their own against color photos).

☐ You wouldn't want to do business with the person in the photo (i.e., your demeanor reads as unpleasant, shady, slick, wacky).

☐ Your photo is more than three years old.

☐ People would not recognize you from your photo.

The quality of your headshot is hugely important – as the first piece of your profile that people notice, it is the way people will remember you. Every time you leave a comment on LinkedIn, send a note to a friend through LinkedIn or someone searching finds your profile, the first thing people will notice is your photo. Make sure it is outstanding. If you do need a new photo, only a professional shot will do. Even so, not every professional photographer will be able to produce a photo worthy of being an executive LinkedIn portrait.

Attributes of an executive-branded LinkedIn portrait

- It is a headshot. When it is cropped for use on LinkedIn, it could also include your shoulders.
- Both your eyes and your mouth should be genuinely smiling and/or you should look approachable. This is your welcome and you want it to be a warm one.
- You should be wearing the kind of clothes you would wear when presenting to your board or executive leadership team.
- If your place of business is your backdrop, the background should be in soft focus so that it does not compete with your face for prominence.
- If the photo is shot at a studio, there should be sufficient contrast between your hair color and the background so that you clearly stand out.
- The photographer has used a make-up artist/ image consultant and/or digital correction to produce an image that is your most flattering look.

Finding the right photographer

You want a photographer who specializes in executive business portraits. Photographers working for big-box stores or the photo department of a retail store will not be likely to produce the quality of photo you require. You want a photographer with a significant portfolio of executive headshots that are enormously appealing to you. When you've identified a few candidates, look at their online portfolios to see if they produce consistently outstanding images. The photographer has no online portfolio? Keep on looking!

Everyone – yes, including men – looks better on camera if they have professionally applied makeup. (Think about on-air talent such as news anchors. They do not go on air barefaced.) If the photographer is not using a make-up artist, make sure that the photographer will digitally touch up the photo you receive.

When you make your appointment with your chosen photographer, tell them that you want their business package. That is, you want pricing for a photo shoot that will produce a number of business headshots to pick from, and a single touched-up image of your choice that you will receive digitally. Unless you also want prints for gifts or your publicity file, tell the photographer that the product you are looking for is a digital image that you have the right to use for LinkedIn and other business purposes.

> Never underestimate the value of an executive-branded LinkedIn portrait.

Resources

Amy Cuddy, *Presence: Bringing Your Boldest Self to Your Biggest Challenges*. New York: Little, Brown and Company, 2015.

Jenna Goudreau, "A Harvard psychologist says people judge you based on two criteria when they first meet you," *Business Insider*, January 16, 2016.

Ty Kiisel, "You Are Judged by Your Appearance," *Forbes*, March 20, 2013.

CHAPTER 4

BEFORE YOU GET TO THE STARTING GATE...

> Unless you've changed your Privacy Settings, your profile may be sending distress signals, advertising your competition and disclosing your entire connections list.

CAROL KAEMMERER

LINKEDIN'S PRIVACY & SETTINGS can undermine the efforts of the most earnest executive by making you appear unable to manage your personal brand. So I recommend that you change the default for the three most troublesome settings.

Don't know how to find your LinkedIn Privacy & Settings? They're hidden, of course. Using your computer (not the app on your phone or tablet), look on your toolbar at the far right for a small photo of you (called your avatar). Hover your mouse over your avatar and you'll find that Privacy & Settings is the second from the last option on the dropdown menu.

Still can't find it? LinkedIn's user interface changes often. I recommend searching Google for "where are LinkedIn's privacy & settings?" Google will point you to a number of articles including the specific information you need on LinkedIn's own Help pages. LinkedIn's Help section is hard to navigate although their instructions are generally clear.

Problematic Settings

When you've located your Privacy Settings, look for and change the default settings on these three items or similar-sounding ones. (*Note that LinkedIn changes the names they give to various settings from time to time and the app may differ from the actual LinkedIn site.*)

- Sharing profile edits
- Who can see your connections
- Viewers of this profile also viewed

These three settings can undermine your ability to show that you are in control of your profile and personal brand. Here's how to change the default response for these settings so that they serve, instead of undermine, you.

SHARING PROFILE EDITS

This sounds benign enough, but it's not. This setting sends an announcement to the homepages of your LinkedIn connections for every single change you make to your profile. So if you are tweaking or making updates to your profile, it will send an announcement for every section of your profile that you touch. After about the third announcement (e.g., John has new experience; John has added skills; John has new education…), you will have inadvertently aroused the curiosity of your connections who happen to be following their homepage feeds. By all means, select "NO" so that every edit does not broadcast.

WHO CAN SEE YOUR CONNECTIONS

Pick the option "Only you," which closes your connections list. There are two reasons for this. First, you've spent your career cultivating your personal contacts and you don't need to be sharing the full list with anyone. Second, each new connection you make will be broadcast to your current connections' homepages if you've not changed this setting to "Only you." This is too much information to share: it provides real-time reporting to others about those you are connecting with, and may serve as a competitive intelligence resource for others.

Selecting the "Only you" option does not mean that your connections won't have any idea of who your connections are, it just means that they can't see a complete listing. When looking at your profile, they will be able to see the connections the two of you have in common. If they are looking at the profile of someone with whom they are not connected, they will be able to see which of their own connections (such as you) might be able to introduce them. In this situation, if you are connected to the person they seek an introduction to, your photo and name will be shown, perhaps along with others.

VIEWERS OF THIS PROFILE ALSO VIEWED

If you have not changed this from the default ("YES") a potential customer or executive recruiter when viewing your profile will also see other people who have similar keywords and skills as yours. It doesn't benefit you to showcase your competitors on your profile. After you've seen what this looks like, change this setting to "NO."

A fourth setting of interest is different than the others in that there is more than one right choice, depending on your intent. The setting is: "Profile viewing options." Your choices for "Profile viewing options" are: *a) Your name and*

> To see how the LinkedIn feature "Viewers of this profile also viewed" displays on your profile when others view it, select the blue "View profile as" button below your LinkedIn photo and then select the "Your connections" option that allows you to see your profile as it appears to others. If you can't find this button because they've changed it, conduct a Google search: "view LinkedIn profile as others view it." If you have not yet changed from the default setting, you will see a list of ten people (with headshots and headings) on the right side of your profile.

headline, b) *Private profile characteristics* and c) *Private mode*. For the most part, the best choice is "a" – you should be you. People like to see that you visited their profile, so be you most of the time. But there are times when you'd like to view someone's profile anonymously. For such a circumstance you should change this setting to "c," the private (anonymous) setting. Remember to change it back when you're done with your competitive intelligence session.

At present, if you do not have a Premium account and you have set what others see to either the semi-private or completely private options (b or c), your penalty for not being transparent is that LinkedIn will not share information with you about who is looking at your profile. Being **you** has its rewards.

Do I Need a LinkedIn Premium Account?

Whether you need to upgrade from a basic to a premium account depends on the kind of user you are and whether you're currently taking full advantage of all the basic account offerings. Most users find that the basic features are sufficient for their purposes. Occasionally a user will find that they are attempting to do something that exceeds the limits of the type of account they have. Examples include exceeding the number of searches you can conduct in a given period of time or the number of searches LinkedIn will save for you. If you have gotten a warning message to this effect from LinkedIn, then a paid LinkedIn account may be appropriate for you.

The users who are most likely to benefit from features offered in premium accounts are people who are:

- in job transition
- mining LinkedIn for sales leads
- recruiting talent

Before signing up for a paid account, consider whether the features offered for a specific kind of account will actually be of value to you. LinkedIn changes its premium account names, features and rates fairly often. To find out about the plans currently being offered, click on the Upgrade button on the right side of your LinkedIn toolbar.

In general, the benefits of the various types of paid accounts center on:

- Seeing your viewers = Ability to see the viewers of your profile for the past 90 days (The basic account lets you see the last five people who have looked at your profile)
- Analytics = Additional analytics and additional search filters
- InMail = The privilege of sending a certain number of InMail messages (email that is forwarded through LinkedIn) to people with whom you are not connected

The following questions can be helpful in evaluating various paid LinkedIn account types.

SEEING YOUR VIEWERS

When evaluating the feature 'ability to see viewers of your profile,' consider:

- How many profile views am I getting per week?
- How many times a week am I willing to check my profile views?
- Based on the average number of profile views I get per week and frequency with which I have been checking my profile views, am I missing some people who have been looking at me?

- If you are not missing anyone who has viewed your profile (that is, you look at these analytics frequently enough that you're not missing any viewers) how would being able to see all the people who have viewed your profile within the last 90 days be helpful to you?

- If you are missing some of the people who are looking at your profile, would you rather look at your analytics more often, or pay so that you don't have to monitor your analytics so regularly?

Note that if a user has visited your profile in the anonymous mode, you will not be able to determine their identity regardless of the type of account you have.

ANALYTICS

Premium accounts may provide access to additional analytics and search filters. (An example of additional analytics might be a chart that analyzes distribution of your viewers by company or by location. An example of additional search filters is the ability to search by all Fortune 500 companies at once.) When evaluating whether these features would be helpful to you, consider:

- If you had access to additional analytics regarding the people who viewed your profile, would that make a difference to you?

- If you were able to more precisely and powerfully target your search, would that make a difference to you?
- If the answer is yes to either of the above, do you think the benefit is commensurate with current rates being offered?

InMail

The ability to send InMail to communicate with someone you are not connected to can be helpful especially to people who are in job transition and people who are using the LinkedIn platform to generate sales leads. Another way to communicate with a LinkedIn user with whom you are not connected is through a group each of you is a member of. You can send a private message through the group to any other member of the group. At present, you can do this 15 times a month.

LinkedIn frequently offers the opportunity to try a premium account free for a month. Take advantage of this if such an offer comes your way. If you find that you make great use of the additional features during the month, it may be worthwhile for you to upgrade on a long-term basis.

> Be savvy! Manage your executive brand by controlling your LinkedIn settings.

Resources

Cheryl Conner, "The LinkedIn Settings Mistakes Most People Still Make," *Forbes*, January 25, 2014.

Carol Kaemmerer, "Is Your LinkedIn Profile Sending Distress Signals?" *LinkedIn Pulse*, June 20, 2015.

CHAPTER 5

YOUR EXECUTIVE- BRANDED LINKEDIN TEXT

> **Don't compare yourself with anyone in this world. If you do, you are insulting yourself.**
>
> BILL GATES

WHAT'S DIFFERENT about the executive-branded LinkedIn profile? Isn't it just like any other profile? Yes and no. It does follow all the same conventions; there is no special format for executives. But an executive-branded profile bespeaks excellence in every way. It is complete, clear, authentic and transparent. Let's start from the top. Your photo and your

An executive-branded profile bespeaks excellence in every way. LinkedIn headline together create a powerful brand image that appears each time your profile is found and each time you post. These personal branding elements are the way you will be known and remembered, so it is important to get them right.

> If you skipped Chapter Four on LinkedIn's Privacy Settings, go back now, read it and implement the suggestions. **Don't make any changes to your profile text until you have changed your settings!**

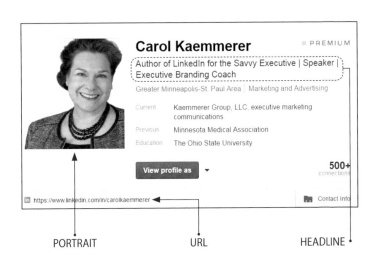

PORTRAIT   URL   HEADLINE

In this chapter, I'm going to cover the main sections of a LinkedIn profile, roughly from top to bottom. The sections are:

- Your executive headline
- Your customized URL (the Internet address for your profile) and other contact information
- Your summary
- Your experience
- Your skills
- Your education
- Optional sections

The LinkedIn portrait, headline, summary and skills are the most central pieces for communicating your personal executive brand. With the exception of the portrait, these are also the sections that take the most time and introspection to complete.

Your executive headline

Your photo and headline together epitomize your personal brand. LinkedIn assigns you a headline that is your current job title and company, but it is possible to customize your headline so it tells the reader much more about you and your brand. Eye-catching headlines are keyword-rich and feature your current or functional title and your unique value proposition. LinkedIn allows 120 characters for your headline and you can communicate a lot within that count.

Your headline is one of the first elements LinkedIn's search algorithm checks for keywords. If you're not familiar with the term "keyword," know that it is actually bit of a misnomer – it's really more like "key search term" because each keyword can be more than one word long. The first keywords you should identify relate to your functional job title – for example, Chief Financial Officer (CFO), Chief Executive Officer (CEO), Vice President (VP).

> Your headline is like a personal advertising slogan.

> Note that for these functional job titles, I listed both the full title and the common abbreviation. This is to hedge your bets. You want to make sure that what ever term the searcher uses to refer to your title, your name will come up. For example, at present a search for Chief Financial Officer will return different results than a search for CFO.

When crafting your headline, brainstorm some other keywords that apply to you. Think about keywords that searchers would use to find someone with your skills. What are your core strengths? Whom and how do you serve? What is different in the work world because of you?

Your headline is like a personal advertising slogan.

- Start with your functional title and some punctuation mark (e.g., a colon or a dash).
- If your company name has strong brand recognition, by all means, use it.
- Round out your 120 characters by answering questions such as:
  - What value do I bring?
  - What is unique about the way I do it?
  - Whom do I serve?

Check out these examples:

Executive Business Coach – What could you achieve if you understood your true purpose?

Senior Sales & Marketing Executive: Mentoring sales leaders | Nurturing customer relationships | Driving record growth

Chief Financial Officer (CFO) – Domestic & international finance | Building strong teams and infrastructure for growth

Medical Device Executive, Medtronic: Outstanding results from concept to commercialization in a global marketplace

Your customized URL and other contact information

A customized URL is an important part of your personal branding. Your URL is the internet address where your profile resides. (*Mine is: https://www.linkedin.com/in/ carolkaemmerer.*) You'll find yours below your portrait. Clicking on the gear icon to the right of your URL will allow you to customize it.

The URL assigned to you by LinkedIn is frustrating to type. It contains your name followed by a string of random, forgettable numbers and letters. The part of the URL you can customize is the portion that follows: "https://www. linkedin.com/in/." Try ending your URL with your name, as I have done. If your name is already taken, some common work-arounds include adding a middle initial, adding academic credentials, using initials for first and middle name or adding a number.

Customize your contact information, consistent with your personal goals. You may include your phone and alternative email addresses. You may also link to up to three websites. If you are currently employed, link to your company's website. Consider featuring your favorite charity as another of the website options.

Your LinkedIn summary

The summary is the most important part of your LinkedIn text. It is where you tell your professional story in 2,000 characters or fewer.

The traits of executive presence – transparency; speaking with passion, energy and knowledge; and connecting with the audience in a strong, positive way – need to shine through your summary. When what you share is authentic, you connect emotionally with your reader. Think of the maxim, "People buy from those they know, like and trust." The more transparent and authentic your profile is, the more people will feel that they like and trust you – and that they'd like to get to know you.

> The traits of executive presence need to shine through your summary.

Here are some steps I use when I write for my executive clients:

> CONSIDER LAST THINGS FIRST.
> As Stephen Covey advises, begin with the end in mind. What do you want to be known for? What are the impressions you want your reader to glean from your LinkedIn profile? Write down three key things. These will begin your list of keywords. Each section of your profile

should use your keywords and reinforce what you want people to remember about you.

HAVE A CONVERSATION.

For your LinkedIn text to connect emotionally with your reader, you have to write conversationally using the first person (i.e., use the word "I" to refer to yourself). Your LinkedIn summary should be the story of your career.

Consider using a story arc to organize your text. For example:

- How have your prior positions informed where you are now and where you're going as a professional?
- Did you come up through the ranks in a specific industry so that you know about all the jobs along the way?
- Have you had the same function in a number of industries, so that your breadth comes from the various industries in which you have worked?

Try using a sentence that starts "I am passionate about..." What comes at the end of that thought? Does it make you smile? If so, it definitely should be part of your LinkedIn summary.

What three things do you want people to remember about you? What are your core principles? How do you motivate people? What are your unique gifts and areas of specialty? What are the accomplishments you want to emphasize?

NOW READ IT ALOUD.

When you are satisfied with your draft, read it out loud. Where did you stumble? Rewrite any sentences that don't read aloud easily. Does the text sound like you? Have you shared your authentic self? Have you conveyed the three key things you want people to know about you? Is it under 2,000 characters? Not yet?

REVISE – AND THEN REVISE AGAIN.

Time spent in creating – and revising – your summary is time well spent. Your summary should convey the essence of the professional you. If the reader of your profile is not intrigued by the time they reach the mid-point of your summary, they'll be on to another profile to find their next collaborator.

Add rich media for increased interest. When you add photos and videos to your summary section, you make your profile more interesting. Include photos of you presenting to an audience, giving or receiving awards or showing your relationship to your business, your employees or your customers. Share company videos that showcase your contribution.

In transition? Consider adding a high-quality video introduction to share your unique value proposition "in person." Video is a perfect medium for capturing your executive presence. While it is also possible to link documents, I recommend against it because documents add no visual value. If you have publications, include them in the Publications section.

Your experience

This is where you get to tell the results of your efforts at each job. List your positions for the last 10 to 15 years. If you want to capture an earlier career experience because it was with a prestigious company or because of its importance to your career, let that be your cut-off point. For each entry, briefly describe the business (unless it's obvious). Help your reader understand the scope of your job by devoting a sentence or two to such things as the number of employees supervised, size of budget or geographies covered.

While you need to enter the year you started and ended your positions, I recommend leaving off the months for a couple of reasons. For some past roles you may not recall the exact month for your start- or end-date. Also, when months are omitted, time spent in transition is more difficult to pinpoint, which may be an advantage.

Using bullet points, list the accomplishments or results that make you the most proud. These are the details that add substance and color to your profile. Remember:

- Use your keywords often.
- Reinforce the things you want people to remember about you.
- Employ powerful verbs.
- Use metrics such as time reduced, savings realized, percent growth or return on investment.
- If you were part of a leadership team responsible for changes, acknowledge that.
- Be gracious: share credit with others. The fact that others were involved doesn't diminish you or your contribution, and not acknowledging others' contributions may cause resentment.

You have 2,000 characters available to address each position. For your more recent positions, using nearly all these characters is to your advantage because the more you write, the more times your keywords will appear in your text. Text that is keyword-dense will help you rank well on a keyword search.

Positions held earlier in your career deserve less attention and hence less text. Be strategic about what you select to highlight. Mention results that relate most closely to activities you might like to do and skills you might like to use in future positions.

List the accomplishments or results that make you the most proud.

You may add effective media (e.g., appropriate photos and video) for each of your positions. If you've got it, share it.

Skills

LinkedIn allows you to list 50 skills from their skills database. Listing the maximum number of skills works to your advantage because skills and keywords go hand-in-hand. Think about how you express your executive presence and personal brand. Make sure that in addition to technical or subject-matter skills you also list some of your softer skills such as those relating to management style, people skills or the ability to accomplish initiatives cross-functionally.

Taking a deep dive into skills on LinkedIn is no small task. It's hard because there is no list of skills to print out and study. Rather, you enter a keyword and see what skills LinkedIn has cataloged under that keyword. For example, if you are results-oriented, you might enter "results." LinkedIn returns a number of options:

- driving results
- driven by results
- achieving measurable results
- bottom-line results
- financial results
- payment by results

Several of these might apply. If getting results is one of your key distinguishers, you might select these options: driving results, achieving measurable results and financial results.

When you've identified your 50 skills, order them so that the skills you want to be known for appear at the beginning of your skills inventory, while similar-sounding skills are listed further down. The skills at the top of the list are the most likely to attract endorsements.

How do your skills get endorsed? Many endorsements will come to you naturally as your colleagues visit your profile. LinkedIn helps out (seemingly randomly) by suggesting in a note at the top of all connections' profiles that they might want to endorse one of their connections for specific skills. Unfortunately, LinkedIn may suggest that people endorse you for skills you have not selected for yourself. Know that you are free **not** to accept endorsements – in fact, you might decide to reject endorsements for skills you did not select to show on your profile. We'll get to more about endorsements in Chapter Nine.

Education

In addition to listing the institutions of higher learning you attended, indicate the degree you earned. If no degree is listed, the reader will assume that you did not earn one. You can also list activities you pursued while attending. It may seem long ago and far away, but if your activities give the reader a window into your tenacity and drive or enduring interests, consider adding them. You are not required to list dates of attendance or graduation. Many executives opt to leave off their graduation dates to make estimating their age more difficult.

You may have taken various courses or management training while employed that were not part of a degree program. These don't fit well in the Education section. Rather, you can enter these in an optional section called "Courses." When you enter a date, the courses are linked to the position you held at the time you took the course. If you hold certifications, list them in the optional "Certifications" section.

Optional sections

Look through the optional sections available to you and see what else you might add. These sections are hidden below your portrait. Look for the "See More" button. Three that almost everyone can add are:

- Volunteer Activities
- Interests
- Advice for Contacting

In the "Volunteer Activities" section, list those activities for which you've used your professional skills on a *pro bono* basis (such as serving as an officer or board member of a non-profit) or the organizations to which you have been truly committed and for which you have spent a considerable amount of time volunteering. For example, a once-a-year, three-hour stint packing meals for a cause probably should not find its way to your profile, but being a trainer of therapy dogs should because of the time and passion it requires.

I always recommend adding an "Interests" section because it offers a look at a different side of you and makes you more authentic – more human and approachable. Write this section in first person.

The "Advice for Contacting" section is a great place to add your email and/or phone number to make it easier for people to connect with you. (You probably entered this information in your Contact Information section, but in order to access that section, the person needs to be one of your connections.) If you're not interested in being contacted, feel free to leave this off.

LinkedIn has many other optional sections that can be added to help tell your story, including:

- Projects
- Organizations
- Honors/Awards
- Patents

- Certifications
- Publications
- Languages

Use as many of the optional sections as applicable to round out and add interest to your professional and personal story.

However, don't add the Languages section if you speak only one language; people understand that you speak the language in which you've written your profile. If you do speak additional languages, be sure to list your primary language as well. There are drop downs to indicate your level of proficiency with each of your listed languages.

> You will be known and remembered by your LinkedIn profile. Take the time to craft a great one.

Resources

Carol Kaemmerer, "Getting Your Ducks in a Row: A Primer on LinkedIn Skills," *LinkedIn Pulse*, April 15, 2015.

CHAPTER 6

STRATEGIES FOR A CONFIDENTIAL JOB SEARCH

> **If you are conducting a confidential job search, don't let LinkedIn be your 'tell.'**

CAROL KAEMMERER

YOU'D LIKE TO prepare yourself for a confidential search for a new position – or maybe you just want to be ready should an opportunity present itself. Perhaps you've already missed an opportunity because your personal marketing collaterals (LinkedIn, résumé, etc.) were not in good order. You know you aren't a good candidate for that next opportunity if your LinkedIn profile is bare, but if you go from bare to all there, won't you attract suspicion?

Yes, it's likely that people will notice when your LinkedIn presence becomes more robust. But here are some things you can do (and not do) that will help keep your job search cards close to your vest.

Be prepared

Your colleagues and staff may comment that your profile is suddenly more complete, so have a response at the ready. You may be able to say truthfully that you have noticed that potential clients check out your profile before meeting you, and you're concerned that your bare-bones profile does not reflect well on you or the company. As personal branding guru, William Arruda, points out, having a well-appointed profile is not just for job seekers; employees who look good on LinkedIn reflect well on their employers.

Specific strategies for confidential job searches

CHANGE PROBLEMATIC SETTINGS.
Go back to Chapter Four to read about and change the three most problematic settings:

- "Who can see your connections"
- "Viewers of this profile also viewed"
- "Sharing profile edits"

Be strategic in changing the setting "Profile viewing options" (*also covered in Chapter Four.*)

GIVE YOUR CURRENT EMPLOYER GOOD VALUE.
If you are currently employed, of course you owe your employer your best efforts during

business hours. Conduct your search on your own time with your own resources. If you are updating your LinkedIn profile, link your company's website to your profile and "Follow" your company. Be familiar and compliant with your company's social media policy.

If you have your company email already visible on your profile (for example, in your Summary or Advice for Contacting sections), don't change it. Doing so would be a clue that you are considering other opportunities. While it is fine to enter your personal email along with your company email in your Contact section (visible only to your connections), I would not add your personal email address elsewhere on your profile at this time, because it could raise eyebrows. (Note that if you are **not** employed, do display your email and/or phone.)

When writing about your current work experience, don't lapse into past tense. Don't hint at your availability or interest in moving to a new position. Speaking badly about your company in person or in writing is never a winning scenario.

HIDE JOB SEARCH-RELATED GROUPS.

It's perfectly fine to join Jobs for CFOs-type groups, but change the settings for those groups so that they are not visible on your profile.

FOLLOW ONLY YOUR CURRENT EMPLOYER.

Don't "Follow" any additional companies at this time unless they are a current client or vendor. Your action of following another company will broadcast. Your colleagues will wonder.

WHAT YOU POST ON LINKEDIN IS PUBLIC.

On your home page and in your group comments, be gracious and discrete. Expect that your boss and HR person may see your LinkedIn activity. Use the platform to your advantage.

RECOMMENDATIONS CAN BE IMPORTANT, BUT...

Don't ask your current boss or colleagues for LinkedIn recommendations during a confidential search. Past colleagues and managers are safer.

HIGHLIGHT YOUR SUBJECT-MATTER EXPERTISE.

Your LinkedIn profile is a personal marketing document, which provides an effective way to keep your name in front of your most important audience. It can be an invaluable tool in the job search. Keep it current. Always put your best foot forward using warm, inviting text that highlights your business passions.

Make good use of your keywords. Share your real self. (*Follow the best practices for an executive-branded LinkedIn profile as outlined in Chapter Five.*)

Ironically, the most powerful searches *do not start in the search box, but rather, to the right of the search box* where you should find and click on the word "Advanced." Clicking on "Advanced" opens a search page that allows you to specify what kind of search you'd like to do (e.g., searching for people, jobs, companies, groups, etc.). You can enter keywords, company names and even narrow the search to a particular geography. To do a geographic-specific job search, choose Location (near the bottom of the page), select "Located in or near" and then enter a zip code in the Postal Code box. LinkedIn will search within a designated number of miles of the zip code you entered. If you do not specify a postal code, you will be conducting a national search.

Demonstrate your thought leadership.

Carefully select and post articles by others that are within your area of subject-matter expertise. Add value through your introductory comments (known as curation of content). If you are an excellent writer, consider publishing your own work on LinkedIn Pulse, within the parameters established by your firm's social media policy.

Let LinkedIn do some of the heavy lifting.

LinkedIn has an excellent search engine that can be enormously helpful to you in identifying target companies and jobs – and in researching people within the company.

Here are some of the ways to use the Advanced Search function to your advantage:

- To search for jobs.
- To search for executive recruiters who recruit in your specialty. Invite them to connect with you.
- To search both nationally (without a zip code) and locally by adding a postal code.
- If you save your searches, LinkedIn will notify you of new postings that match your search criteria.

- When you find an opportunity you would like to pursue, use LinkedIn to research people within your network who know about the company as well as those who will be interviewing you.

> When used strategically, your LinkedIn profile is your best marketing tool for landing your next great work adventure.

Resources

William Arruda, "18 Reasons Why You Need Every Employee Using LinkedIn Every Day," *Forbes*, April 19, 2015.

William Arruda, "Why Every Employee at Your Company Should Use LinkedIn," *Forbes*, January 7, 2014.

CHAPTER 7

BE SAVVY ABOUT BUILDING YOUR NETWORK

> **Look for connections who can help you build your desired network, but ALWAYS focus on bringing your network QUALITY and VALUE!**
>
> JEROME KNYSZEWSKI

WHO SHOULD BE in my network?" I get asked this question every time I speak to a group or work with a new client. There are as many answers to this question as there are people asking it. The answer depends on your goals, how you wish to use LinkedIn and your own leadership style.

You are probably sitting on a mound of LinkedIn invitations right now that you don't know what to do with. Many people will send you connection requests just because of your position. Why not ignore them all? Because you're better than that. You need a thoughtful approach. Here are some principles that can help you sort through those invitations and guide you in crafting your own answer to "who should be in my network?"

DIVERSITY IS A GOOD THING.

Some executives only connect to people they know well and who are at the same level within their organization. On the face of it, this seems a reasonable strategy, but by refusing all other invitations you may miss opportunities. Don't reject all invitations from strangers out of hand.

Because…

Perhaps the stranger who sent you an invitation is on a search committee for a board; by not responding you may have already failed the test. Also, if your personal brand involves employee focus, what message are you sending when you fail to respond to an invitation sent by a gung-ho millennial employee or a secretary within your company? Just as a garden in which all the flowers are the same height and color is boring, a network comprised only of your peers will not expose you to different points of view that may be interesting and helpful.

SIZE MATTERS.

Keeping your network small does not serve you well.

Because...

One of the two main factors that drives LinkedIn's search algorithm is your relationship to the person who is searching. Therefore, other things being equal, LinkedIn's search algorithm favors people with large networks. Why should you care about being found through a LinkedIn keyword search? Because people are using LinkedIn to check out individuals when looking for a partner for a new venture, or a new board member or executive.

> Strong leaders build wide networks.

REFLECT YOUR NATURAL SOCIAL SPHERE.

Because...

You are not one-dimensional. Don't just look across and up. Strong leaders build wide networks. Consider:

- Who are your customers? Are they external? Internal? Both? Those you serve would be good additions to your network.

- Whom do you supervise? Leaders pay attention to their direct reports and other employees within their organization.

- Who are your colleagues? People you consider colleagues, whether they are inside your company or working elsewhere, are reasonable additions.
- To whom do you report? It is strategic to add these people to your network.
- Who is in your social circle? Yes, it is appropriate to include people you know through your church, children's school and other social situations.

LET YOUR GOALS GUIDE YOU.

Because...

If you are responsible for bringing in new business, a stranger's invitation may be more attractive if it represents a potential new customer. If you are actively cultivating your personal thought leadership, people who respond to your postings (through "Likes," "Comments" or "Shares") may be good additions to your network regardless of who they are because they help disseminate your message. If you are looking for a new opportunity outside your current organization, executive recruiters and people who work for your target companies may become an important part of your network.

WRITE YOUR OWN RULES.
Apply them. Re-evaluate.

Because...

Having criteria that you will use to sort out which invitations you will accept and which you will reject can be very helpful and reduce the amount of time required to hit "Accept" or "Ignore." With clear guidance, you could even delegate accepting LinkedIn invitations to an assistant.

Periodically revisit your rules to make sure they are working for you. I used to reject any invitation that wasn't personalized. But I quickly determined that my rule was causing me to reject the very people I hoped to attract, since many executives are not familiar with how to access the dialog box that allows you to personalize a connection request.

DECLINE GRACIOUSLY.
Not everyone is a good fit for your network.

So...

Hitting the "Ignore" button is a perfectly legitimate response, but if you'd like to be more gracious, here is a response LinkedIn guru and author, Wayne Breitbarth, suggests that I frequently use: *"Thanks for asking me to join your LinkedIn network. I typically don't accept people into my network until I have either met them or understand how we might be able to help each other. So let me know how we might be able to collaborate. I look forward to hearing from you."*

In addition to responding to invitations, you should also reach out to people you enjoy and to those who have been important to your career over time. *How to do this effectively is the topic of our next chapter.*

> Building a strong network that goes beyond your organization (both on LinkedIn and in person) is a vital career strategy for savvy executive leaders.

Resources

Wayne Breitbarth, "Is Opportunity Knocking at Your LinkedIn Door?" *Power Formula*, June 12, 2016.

CHAPTER 8

CULTIVATING YOUR CONNECTIONS, WITH CLASS

Make your invitation better than a robo message.

CAROL KAEMMERER

BUILDING A STRONG LinkedIn network is not just a matter of responding to invitations. You will also want to extend invitations to valued business connections and cultivate those relationships with care.

The invitation to connect

Your invitation to someone really does need to be personalized, even if you know the person well. Doing things the right way is part of your executive presence. A personalized invitation shows respect to the person you are inviting and demonstrates your own civility. Perhaps you already understand that. You may intend to send a personal invitation, but then you click the "Connect" button and, like magic, a robo-invitation is sent. You've lost your opportunity to make a great impression.

HOW DO ROBO-INVITATIONS HAPPEN?

How does a robo-invitation get sent? It happens when you click "Connect" from a "People You May Know" gallery or some other list that LinkedIn has presented to you, or when you are using a LinkedIn app on your phone or tablet. There are some obscure ways to get the LinkedIn-presented listings or the app to allow you to personalize a message, but your best bet is to send invitations from your computer as described below.

HOW CAN I BE SURE I CAN PERSONALIZE MY INVITATION?

The never-fail method is:

- Navigate to the person's profile on your computer.
- From their profile, click "Connect."
- The dialogue box will appear to indicate how you know the person and give you the opportunity to write an appropriate invitation.

Connecting from the person's profile allows you to review their profile for commonalities, making your personalized invitation even stronger. You might find new common ground with long-time business associates. Most people are flattered when someone reviews their profile, which gives you a leg up on that good impression you intend to make.

Some executives have no problem in the introductory part of the invitation but are unsure of the words to use in the asking part of the invitation. A phrase that I have often used is, *"I would be delighted to have you join my LinkedIn network."* Whatever words you choose, offer your LinkedIn invitations with grace and style.

Cultivating your connections

Associate authentically with the people you'd like to cultivate as professional friends or prospective employees, business partners or customers. Your connections are not chips to amass to win some grand career game. They are real people, whom you might enjoy getting to know better.

The most visible and universally appreciated strategy for nurturing a relationship on LinkedIn is to pay attention to what your target connections are posting and respond with a "Comment," "Share" or "Like."

You'll find "Like," "Comment" and "Share" buttons below the photo associated with the post. (*For more information about engaging with content on the homepage, see Chapter Ten.*)

There are several other ways for cultivating your online relationships, including:

- Visit their profile – without doing anything else. It's really quite amazing that just showing up on the list of people who visited their profile actually increases friendly feelings.

- Endorse a few of the skills you have observed or can intuit by reading their profile. Endorse just a few so that you can return and add a few more at a future time.

- Ask them a question about something that interests you that is in their area of expertise. People like to share their knowledge.

- Write them a recommendation. However, you really need to know the person well and have seen them in action to do this.

- Share an article with them that you think they'd find interesting.

- Provide or ask for an introduction.

- Send them a message.

- Invite them to coffee or to chat by phone.

Cultivate your connections by engaging amiably and bringing value. Get ready to see the world through a different lens!

CHAPTER 9

WHAT ABOUT RECOMMENDA- TIONS AND ENDORSE- MENTS?

> When you say it, it's marketing.
> When your customer says
> it, it's social proof.
>
> ANDY CRESTODINA

"**S**OCIAL PROOF" is an indication of support from other people. LinkedIn uses two forms of social proof: recommendations and endorsements. Recommendations are just what you'd expect: they are like a written letter of reference. A meaningful recommendation takes considerable time and effort to be done well.

An endorsement of skills, on the other hand, takes little effort. It's a matter of clicking a plus sign on someone else's profile to indicate which of their skills you would like to endorse. It's not unusual for people who have little knowledge of your skills to endorse you. Understand such an endorsement as a way for a person to say "hello."

For each of these types of social proof, you must decide:

- Will you seek (or accept) them for yourself?
- Will you provide them for others?

Your decisions, and how you implement them, should be consistent with how you define your personal brand and executive presence. Define for yourself a set of rules you will follow and be willing to articulate those rules so that they make sense to others.

Recommendations

WILL YOU SEEK RECOMMENDATIONS FOR YOURSELF?

Recommendations, whether they come from a boss, peer or subordinate, can be powerful testimonies to your effectiveness and how you relate to people. When recommendations come to you unsolicited, receive them as the blessing they are. LinkedIn allows you to review the recommendation and request revisions. Take advantage of this and read through the recommendation carefully. A typo or other error can undermine the effectiveness of a recommendation and be a source of embarrassment to both you and the recommender. Tactfully ask your recommender to make changes if they are needed. When you're comfortable with it, add the recommendation to your profile. Always send a note of thanks via LinkedIn or in another way that best represents your personal executive presence.

But should you request recommendations? Recommendations for executives who are well into their career are probably less important than they are for newer executives. Being hired for multiple executive roles over time serves as its own form of social proof.

> When recommendations come to you unsolicited, receive them as the blessing they are.

For executives who would like to be recommended, know that requesting a recommendation from people related to your current position may raise concerns about your future job plans. It is safer to request recommendations from bosses or colleagues who have left the company or are related to past positions.

Be prepared for the possibility that the person from whom you are requesting a recommendation has a practice of not writing recommendations for posting on the internet. If you encounter a pushback of that sort, try not to take it personally.

LL YOU PROVIDE RECOMMENDATIONS
R OTHERS?

e decisions you make about writing recommendations for others must be evaluated
against the way you have chosen to express
your executive presence, so think this through.
How will you respond if you are requested to
provide a recommendation for a person you
admire who fits one of these categories?

- A current or former colleague
- A current or former direct report
- A current or former superior
- A vendor

If you choose to write a recommendation, know
that:

- It is the nicest gift you could give someone,
  and very valuable for their career.
- It will take a chunk of time for you to do it well.
- What you write and how you write it will
  reflect on you.
- It will last forever.
- Others will ask that you recommend them
  as well, citing prior recommendations you
  have written.

Make sure that you can articulate and support your rationale about those for whom you
will and will not write recommendations, and

One tactful way to deliver a negative response is saying something like...

"I am happy to be a reference for you by phone. If I can respond to someone's questions directly about your appropriateness for a particular position based on what I know about you, I'll be happy to do that. But once I start writing recommendations for *[insert the category of people you've decided not to write for]*, I open myself up to too many requests to handle. So, I've had to make a personal policy decision to handle requests for recommendations *[perhaps add category here]* in this way."

deliver your message kindly. If you are a popular boss who has just left the company, know that many people may clamor for a recommendation from you. Be ready with a response.

Endorsements

WILL YOU SEEK ENDORSEMENTS FOR YOURSELF?

I don't generally recommend requesting endorsements. But if you are in transition, you might ask close friends to endorse a few of your top skills. Whenever you receive an endorsement, send a polite note of thanks via LinkedIn. Endorsing others is one way to garner more endorsements, but know that many people will neither acknowledge your endorsement nor reciprocate.

Endorsements can only be given by someone with whom you are connected. Interestingly, the skill being endorsed does not have to appear on your profile. LinkedIn may suggest that others endorse you for skills that they deem to be consistent with the skills you have listed on your profile. If you are endorsed for a skill that's not on your skills inventory, feel free accept it (and it will be added) or reject it. Your endorser will not be alerted that you've decided not to list the skill. Acknowledge with gratitude, regardless. Something like *"Thanks for thinking of me and endorsing my skills"* should suffice.

It is also possible to set up your skills section so that it will not accept endorsements. If you are among the professionals who are subject to regulatory restrictions that prohibit the display of endorsements (e.g., financial advisors), or if you'd just prefer not to show endorsements on your profile, make use of this option.

WILL YOU PROVIDE
ENDORSEMENTS FOR OTHERS?

This is such a simple thing to do that the answer should surely be "yes." Do it strategically. When you're thinking of someone or you'd like them to be thinking of you, visit their profile and thoughtfully endorse three skills. This allows you to revisit their profile at another time to endorse a few more.

> Recommendations and endorsements on LinkedIn can build your online network and cultivate your connections. Use and accept them thoughtfully.

Resources

Andy Crestodina, "The Psychology of Social Proof & How to Build Trust in Your Business," *Unbounce,* October 9, 2013.

CHAPTER 10

HOW OFTEN SHOULD I POST?

> Social media is changing the way we communicate and the way we are perceived, both positively and negatively. Every time you post a photo, or update your status, you are contributing to your own digital footprint and personal brand.

AMY JO MARTIN

AM USING the verb "post" loosely here to include all your interactions with your connections and with articles through your LinkedIn homepage (the page where you see people commenting on articles). This interaction includes:

- Liking, commenting on and sharing material that has previously been shared by others
- Sharing a status update, which includes sharing an article with your comments (a.k.a. curating an article), sharing a photo, noting that you'll be attending a conference, etc.
- Writing a long-form post (i.e., your own article that you publish on LinkedIn Pulse)

How often should you post? Just like the answer to who should be in your network, the answer to how often you should post depends on your personal goals. I suggest that you spend some time each day interacting on LinkedIn. You'll soon find a comfortable rhythm and begin to engage more freely. Participating in the conversation can be quite strategic. Many executives who curate content on a regular basis find it is an excellent way to demonstrate their thought leadership and engage with others.

> Spend some time each day interacting on LinkedIn.

Rather than being prescriptive about how many articles you should share or how many comments you should offer each week, I suggest a time-oriented goal. Start with five minutes a day and ramp up, as appropriate, depending on your objectives. People who should spend more time on LinkedIn are those who want to:

- Actively promote their company and/or brand
- Share their thought leadership

- Be available for new opportunities
- Nurture relationships with their connections (who may also be their customers or clients)

Ways to get involved in the homepage conversation:

WATCH AND FEEL THE RHYTHM.

Your LinkedIn homepage can feel like an intimidating place to be. I suggest that you be an observer at first. You can't know what to do without seeing how others do it. Perhaps someone in your network seems particularly adept at posting interesting articles and commenting on others' posts. Do you like what they do? If so, use them as a role model.

Remember that every response you make on your homepage is public. It can be seen on the homepage of each of your connections and potentially beyond. Be aware that the LinkedIn homepage is not the place to chat or arrange a tee time (as I have seen done!). When you think you've got the rhythm, you're ready for your online move.

START SMALL.

A "Like" (the thumbs-up icon) is an easy place to start. A "Like" moves the article or comment to your connections' homepages so that they can see it too. It is also a compliment to the person who originally posted.

> **WHAT YOUR CONNECTIONS SEE**
>
> *Your LinkedIn portrait and name beside the statement "[Your name] likes:" The content you "Liked" will appear below that.*

Some people consistently share good content; you'll find them over time. When you scroll quickly through your homepage feed, look for these people, as well as your friends and others who interest you, such as your customers, your employees or people you'd like to know better. Responding to what others post, even with a "Like," is a way to further a relationship.

MOVE UP TO A COMMENT.

Think about why you found an article interesting or identify some point that was particularly noteworthy and "Comment" on that. Aim for saying something that would make your connections interested in reading the article (i.e., something more profound and on-point than *"Nice!"*).

> **WHAT YOUR CONNECTIONS SEE**
>
> *Your LinkedIn portrait and name beside the statement "[Your name] commented on:" The content you commented on will appear below that.*

Commenting is a way to nurture your onli relationships. Remember that what you s and how you interact online is part of the public record and reflects on your personal brand. As your mother probably told you, *"If you don't have anything nice to say, don't say anything at all."* There is too much negativity in the world already.

Depending on how many comments the article or graphic attracts, your connections may or may not be able to see what you wrote, even though they see that you commented. To make sure the person who posted originally sees your comment, hyperlink their name in your post (called tagging). This is both tactful and strategic, since it supports your contact and ensures that they can view your post. (*For good instructions on how to do this, google "how to tag someone on LinkedIn."*)

SHARE AND CURATE.

You can share your own thoughts in a status up-date by clicking the "Share an update" section of your homepage. You can also share another author's article or photo with your commentary (known as curating). When you share someone else's article, be sure to give credit to the author by hyperlinking their name (tagging).

> ### WHAT YOUR CONNECTIONS SEE
>
> *Your LinkedIn portrait, name and headline with the content appearing below that.*
>
> *If you provided an introduction to the content, your remarks will appear between your headline and the content.*

Curating content (by sharing content with your commentary) is an especially powerful way to convey your thought leadership. You have identified good content and provided commentary to suggest to others why they should read it. Your introduction will not get buried by comments from others as it might if you simply added a comment to the post. If you tag the original author they may respond to you, giving both your commentary and their article additional exposure.

WRITE YOUR OWN LONG-FORM POSTS.

Consider this only if you love to write and feel you have important content to contribute. Although it is relatively easy to publish on LinkedIn, that does not mean that you should write casually. What you say and how you say it reflects on you and your brand, so this is not a place for text-speak (e.g., R U going?) or material that is not carefully written. If writing is not your forte, then skip this strategy.

Engaging with others

You can use all the LinkedIn strategies described above (*and in Chapter Eight*) as a way to nurture your online relationships. Set a goal for yourself to review your LinkedIn homepage daily, contributing a few "Likes" and "Comments" with each visit. Make a point to curate and "Share" something you found insightful, several times a week. If someone comments on something you shared, respond to them – always cordially.

Why is it important to "Like," "Comment" and "Share?"

When you interact with material that someone else has previously posted with a "Like," "Comment" or "Share," you give your network access to that content on their homepages. It also associates your name with content you think has merit. Liking a friend's content is a way to affirm the connection between the two of you. Remember to give credit to the person who shared and/or the author by hyperlinking (or tagging) their names.

Cultivating personal thought leadership

For those seeking to communicate their personal brand online, LinkedIn is a wonderful place to do so. It's easier than you might think to consistently convey what you stand for without writing long-form posts. To find on-point articles to share, think of keywords or phrases that define your personal brand and create a Google Alert for each of them. (*Search for Google Alert and follow the* seeking to communicate their personal brand online, LinkedIn is a wonderful place to do so. *directions to create an alert.*) Every day, Google will automatically search for articles pertinent to your alerts and will send you links to relevant articles. Your job is to evaluate whether an article is worthy of sharing and if so, to curate it by writing commentary that would entice your connections to read it.

How should I allocate the time I spend on LinkedIn?

- Each day, reply to comments directed to you. LinkedIn will notify you of comments on your recent posts. Be courteous and thank the commenter.

- Scroll through your homepage looking for articles or particular connections that catch your eye. Skim the article or other material and determine how you might "Share" the article in a way that reinforces your brand, or encourage your connection with a "Like" or "Comment."

- Curate and post articles pertinent to your personal brand. How often you do this will depend on how intent you are on demonstrating your thought leadership.

- Once a week, send notes of thanks to your new connections. Whether you invited them or they invited you, starting a new online relationship by expressing gratitude is a classy thing to do.

- Once a week, respond to connection requests you have received. Visit the person's profile and determine whether to connect or not, depending on whether they fit the criteria you've set for people in your network.
- Once a month, send invitations to people you'd like to welcome to your network.
- If you are in job transition, you should spend time every day on the activities noted above.

What should I do when I find distasteful material on my homepage?

Most people understand that LinkedIn is a professional site and that some material that might be tolerated or even enjoyed on Facebook is not appropriate to post on LinkedIn. Kitten videos, math puzzles, word games, suggestive photos, etc., fall into this category. Obviously, you should steer clear of this type of material on LinkedIn.

But if you respond online to poor quality content in any way (even to chide others for their inappropriate posts), your photo, name, headline – and reputation – become associated with it. If the content offends you so deeply that you cannot ignore it, consider any of the strategies listed below, but don't engage with objectionable content on your homepage.

Here are some more appropriate responses:

- Privately contact the connection who posted the material. They may have actually been commenting on the inappropriateness of the post and not realize that by their comment they are sending the objectionable material on to you and others.
- Disconnect with the connection who posted the material. (*Go to your Connections tab. On your connections list, find the person you wish to disconnect with and click "Remove."*)
- Hide all the posts from that individual so that they will no longer be visible on your homepage. (*Move your cursor to the upper right side of the post to see the down arrow. "Hide this particular post" and "Unfollow [name of the person who posted]" are among the options here.*)

> Make it a habit to interact on LinkedIn each day, using each visit strategically to enhance your personal brand.

Resources

Carol Kaemmerer, "Jump into the LinkedIn Conversation," *LinkedIn Pulse*, March 8, 2016.

Carol Kaemmerer, "Ten Gracious Ways to Say Hello on LinkedIn," *LinkedIn Pulse*, September 15, 2014.

CHAPTER 11

BRINGING IT ALL TOGETHER

> To be in business today, our
> most important job is to be
> head marketer for the
> brand called YOU.
>
> TOM PETERS

TOP EXECUTIVES whose LinkedIn profile does not reflect well on them miss out when…

- High-potential talent checks them out as a prospective employer and then selects another company.

- Possible business collaborators decide they'll look elsewhere.

- Prospective customers or clients select others who have articulated their value proposition with authenticity and transparency.

ream opportunity goes instead to a peer who
ʒages daily with colleagues on LinkedIn.

As New York Times best-selling author and Fortune 500 consultant Dan Schawbel has said, "Your personal brand serves as your best protection against business factors you can't control."

> As a savvy executive, you can – and should – take control of your online reputation.

It matters what your LinkedIn photo looks like, what your LinkedIn profile says, and how you use the platform to cultivate your relationships and communicate your thought leadership. So as we bring this book to a close, test your updated profile against the following checklists.

A savvy executive LinkedIn profile

Basics (Chapters 2, 4, 5)

☐ I have customized my settings so that LinkedIn does not broadcast every profile edit I make, my profile does not advertise my competition and I am not exposing my connections list.

☐ I've asked a trusted colleague to help me proof my content for grammar and typographical errors.

☐ If I am currently employed, a link to my company's website is associated with my account. If I am in transition, a link to my former employer's website is not associated with my account.

☐ I have identified my keywords and used them often in my profile text.

☐ If a stranger spent two minutes looking at my profile, they could recall key things about me.

☐ My profile is "complete" – it has a customized headline and URL, a summary that tells my business story, an experience section that includes my results in each position (going back at least ten years) and my education.

☐ I have used some additional sections to tell my story such as volunteer activities, interests, honors, etc.

☐ I have used rich media (photos, videos, etc.) to add interest to my profile.

☐ My colleagues would recognize this profile as mine, even without my photo or name.

☐ I am pleased with how my personal brand and executive presence are represented in my profile.

My portrait (Chapter 3)

☐ My portrait was taken by a professional photographer.

☐ My portrait is a head or head-and-shoulders shot with an approachable expression.

☐ My portrait is less than three years old and still looks like me.

☐ In my portrait, I am dressed as I would be for a board presentation.

☐ A stranger could recognize me from my portrait.

☐ When I see my portrait it makes me smile.

My headline (Chapter 5)

☐ My headline has been customized for maximum impact within the 120 characters allowed. It includes my functional title and keywords that address my unique value proposition.

☐ My headline is easy to say aloud without stumbling.

☐ My headline is focused; I have not included every role I could possibly perform.

☐ If I were a product, my headline could be used as a marketing tagline.

☐ When I read my headline, it makes me proud.

My summary (Chapter 5)

☐ I have used almost my full allotment of 2,000 characters to tell my business story.

☐ My keywords are used often in my summary.

☐ My summary is written in first person ("I") and reflects me with authenticity, tact and power.

☐ The things I most want to be known for are featured prominently in my summary.

☐ If my colleagues read my summary, they would say it is spot on.

☐ My summary pleases me. It captures the essence of who I am and the skills, experiences, values and principles I bring to the world of work.

My experience section (Chapter 5)

☐ I have represented my job experience going back 10 to 15 years.

☐ I have seeded my text under each job with my keywords.

☐ My entries for my most recent positions make good use of the 2,000 characters allotted.

☐ My entries include info to help others understand my scope of influence such as number of employees supervised, size of budget, geographies covered, etc.

☐ I've used bullet points to describe my key accomplishments. Where possible, I have used numbers to convey accomplishments such as ROI; increases in sales or production in comparison with prior years; decreases in time, resources, etc.

☐ Rather than being exhaustive in each job description, I have selected those results that relate most closely to activities I might like to do and skills I might like to use in the future.

☐ Where appropriate, I have given credit to my team or others who were important to the successes I cite.

☐ When I review my experience, I am pleased that it represents me well.

My skills (Chapter 5)

☐ I have listed almost 50 skills, including softer skills (e.g., people skills, communication skills) as well as skills that are specific to my industry.

☐ I have ordered my skills so that the top 10 skills listed are the executive expression of the skills I most enjoy using.

☐ I have ordered my skills so that the last 25 skills on my list include those that sound very similar to skills that are higher on the list and are skills that I wouldn't mind using again but are no longer central to what I do.

My education (Chapter 5)

☐ My college and graduate school and degrees achieved are listed. I understand that it is not essential for me to list years attended.

☐ If I attended institutions of higher learning without a degree, I have included the school without listing a degree.

☐ I've listed activities I participated in while at school if they are relevant or particularly interesting.

☐ If I participated in coursework sponsored by my employer, I have listed those courses under the section called Coursework.

☐ If I have earned certifications, I have listed those under the section called Certifications.

Optional sections (Chapter 5)

☐ I have found the dropdown menu with optional sections and have considered and added the sections that help showcase my personal brand with authenticity and transparency.

Hallmarks of savvy use of LinkedIn

Beyond your actual profile, the way you use LinkedIn is also part of your executive branding. Check your own behavior on LinkedIn against this checklist of best practices.

My network and invitations (Chapters 7 and 8)

☐ I understand that having a large network is advantageous for me and that diversity in my network can expose me to broadening viewpoints. I have set some personal rules that are consistent with my personal brand that I use each time I have to decide whether or not to accept an invitation.

☐ I have developed my own guidelines for determining who should be in my network. When I receive an invitation to connect, I can evaluate the requester's appropriateness for my network. My guidelines are consistent with the way I express my executive presence.

☐ I evaluate my guidelines periodically to determine whether they are serving me well.

☐ I always send a personalized invitation as a way to show respect to the person I am inviting to connect.

☐ Whether I initiated or responded to an invitation, I send a follow-up communication of thanks.

Cultivating my connections via LinkedIn (Chapters 8 and 9)

☐ I am strategic when I scan my LinkedIn homepage. I look for those with whom I want to connect. If appropriate to my brand, I will "Like," "Comment" on or "Share" what they have contributed.

☐ When I curate an article or "Comment" on a posting of one of my connections, I give credit by hyperlinking (tagging) the author or poster's name.

☐ When I read an interesting article that is consistent with the brand of one or more of my connections, I send it to them via LinkedIn with a note that I am thinking of them.

☐ I use endorsements strategically as an efficient way of touching others positively.

☐ I know and use several strategies for nurturing my professional relationships online.

☐ I have developed my own guidelines regarding those for whom I will write recommendations and those requests that I will decline. My rationale is easy for me to explain to others and consistent with my expression of personal brand and executive presence.

Cultivating my thought leadership (Chapters 9 and 10)

☐ I always have my personal brand in mind when I "Like," "Comment" on or "Share" material on the LinkedIn homepage.

☐ Through my participation on the homepage, I have identified sources that consistently provide great content.

☐ I know where to find articles that are consistent with my brand. I curate those articles on a regular basis as a way to communicate my personal brand.

☐ I have established a rhythm and frequency for my participation on LinkedIn that is comfortable for me and consistent with my goals.

☐ I do not comment negatively on anyone's posts because I understand that in doing so I am passing along poor content that reflects negatively on my personal brand.

☐ If I enjoy (and am good at) writing my own content, I contribute my own articles through LinkedIn Pulse.

Strategies for a confidential job search (Chapter 6)

☐ I am prepared with a ready response when colleagues ask me about improvements to my LinkedIn profile.

☐ I understand that my activity on LinkedIn could reveal my search, so I have carefully read Chapter Six so that my actions align with my goals.

How does your profile measure up? If it is lacking, review the chapters noted in the checklist. Or consider seeking assistance from a coach skilled in executive branding and the use of LinkedIn.

In closing, I am reminded of Warren Buffet's statement, *"It takes 20 years to build a reputation and five minutes to ruin it. If you think about that, you'll do things differently."*

LinkedIn is a powerful tool to reinforce and communicate your personal executive brand and reputation. Use it wisely and thrive.

ACKNOWLEDGEMENTS

MY PASSION for teaching executives how to own and control their personal brand stems from my observation that age discrimination is alive and well in the workplace. As my talented, senior-level friends and colleagues approached mid-career, their concerns about job security intensified. Many worried that if they lost their job they might never find their way back into the workforce. Indeed, that was my own fear when I was separated from my stable working situation as my business client of twenty years changed to a retained, single-vendor for all their marketing communications.

While mourning the loss of my client in 2011 and struggling to find a way to use my communications talents in another venue, I learned that ranking highly on LinkedIn was not a matter of luck. I learned about the levers that control the search algorithm and discovered the strategies which, when executed with skill, resulted in my being found for other opportunities. I helped many newly-unemployed friends get savvy about LinkedIn before I realized that executive LinkedIn coaching was my ideal next career. It combined my ability to understand and explain technology with my talent for telling business stories with authenticity, tact and power. And, it had the benefit of restoring my clients' confidence and sense of control. Through this book I am hoping to reach a larger audience than my one-on-one consultations allow.

I am grateful to so many who helped me along my journey toward the publication of this book. My wonderful husband and life partner Bill Kaemmerer, who supports me in all things, is always my first editor and touch point. It is a wondrous thing to be loved unconditionally, and even more wonderful to be loved by someone so accomplished in his own scientific career.

My colleague and publisher Richard Dodson, author of *Power Your Career: The Art of Tactful Self Promotion at Work*, was the catalyst for my book. He issued the challenge, gave the book a name, cheered me on and provided publishing know-how. Thanks go also to my editor Gabrielle Dane, who contributed her attention to detail, wordsmithing prowess and formatting skills to make the most important concepts more accessible to my very busy audience.

I am indebted to Jack (John F.) Ruppel, facilitator of the Senior Executive Forum at Lee Hecht Harrison

Minneapolis, who provided many opportunities over several years to speak to and interact with my favorite audience: senior executives. Having the opportunities to both hear Jack's counsel for his tribe and to test the power of my own words and concepts informed the development of the material offered in this book.

To my executive clients, I'd like to express my thanks for the privilege of telling your business stories with passion and authenticity. A little piece of my heart is attached to each profile I write to cheer you on in your career endeavors. I have enjoyed teaching you how to use the LinkedIn platform graciously to nurture your network and convey your thought leadership. My experience working with you has informed both my writing style and content for this book.

I enlisted an army of colleagues, clients and friends to read and comment on my first draft to ensure that my advice was sound and my tone appropriate for executive readers. It was a worthy exercise resulting in the addition of new material and the tweaking of tone, language and formatting to ensure that concepts would be readily grasped. Thanks go especially to my readers whose detailed comments resulted in specific changes: Sue Plaster, M.Ed. of Sue Plaster Consulting; Mary Kloehn of Navigate Forward; Jennifer Kelly of KeliComm Headshots; and executive clients Tony Fisher, retail executive and entrepreneur; Kurt Grotenhuis, CPA of KURT Konsulting; and Bob Thompson, MPA, MS of

Comprehensive Reimbursement Solutions. Other manuscript readers whose kind comments cheered me to the finish line included Mark McCaughey, Lori Syverson, Roshini Rajkumar, Nancy Burke, Eric Gustafson, Sally Stockbridge, Barb Bender and Rob Dalton. I'm especially indebted to my favorite LinkedIn guru Wayne Breitbarth, and brand guru extraordinaire William Arruda.

I am indebted to my book designer, Ivan Stojić, for his clear and elegant style. Thanks also goes to my photographer Jennifer Kelly for capturing my brand through her lens.

It is my hope that the knowledge, skills and strategies I've imparted in this book will empower you to take control of your personal brand online so that you will thrive regardless of any business storms you may encounter.

Carol J. Kaemmerer

ABOUT THE AUTHOR

CAROL J. KAEMMERER loves to tell a good business story. She's been doing so in various ways most of her career.

Since 2011, Carol has focused her communications expertise on helping brand-name leaders and C-suite executives use LinkedIn powerfully, creating positioning and messaging that reflects their true business passion with authenticity. Pairing her marketing flair and ability to communicate with her deep knowledge of the ever-changing LinkedIn platform, she optimizes her clients' ability to be found on this essential social medium. She also teaches clients to use LinkedIn graciously to nurture professional relationships and cultivate thought leadership with their ideal audience.

Carol is a popular speaker and corporate trainer, specializing in how to effectively use LinkedIn as a personal branding and business development tool. Businesses engage Carol to help them have a larger footprint on LinkedIn, to teach about LinkedIn and personal branding, to provide one-on-one coaching to their top executives and to conduct employee workshops. When employees look good on LinkedIn, the company looks good too.

Contact Carol through her website, carolkaemmerer.com or LinkedIn profile, https://www.linkedin.com/in/carolkaemmerer.